The First Adventure of the S.S. Happiness Crew:

CAP'N JOSHUA'S DANGEROUS DILEMMA

By June Dutton

Illustrations by Eric Hill

Determined Productions, Inc.

San Francisco

"That's TOO easy, Papa! ANYONE can blow out ONE candle. I had EIGHT on my birthday—and even THAT was too easy!"

Cap'n Joshua (sometimes called 'Cap'n Josh') laughed. "My cake is a bon voyage cake," he said to his son. "Cakes like this have only one candle. It means, 'Have a happy trip.'"

"Eat your dessert, children," their mother said. "Then you can watch TV."

1

Jenny helped her husband finish packing. Tomorrow he would leave their house on Monterey Bay. Cap'n Joshua would fly to San Francisco, board his ship, the S.S. HAPPINESS, and sail to China, the first stop on a round-the-world cruise that would keep him away from home for six months.

As the children switched on the TV, an announcer was saying, "...and this beautiful boat is the cruise ship S.S. HAPPINESS."

"MAMA, PAPA, COME QUICK," the children shouted. "PAPA'S SHIP IS ON TV!"

"And this is Alice," the announcer went on, "the lucky winner of a round-the-world cruise aboard the S.S. HAPPINESS. Don't be shy, Alice, say hello to everyone, and tell us about yourself and how it feels to win such a grand prize."

"Please," she murmured, "just call me 'Allie.' Everyone does." (Indeed, Allie WAS shy and she had never been on TV before.) "I—uh—work in a library. I know lots about books but not much about boats. The biggest boat I have ever been on is a ferryboat." She smiled shyly.

"Look at that!" said Josh laughing. "Lucky little Allie will be our good luck charm on this trip. What a splendid voyage we will have. A TOAST TO ALLIE!"

At the Monterey county airport the next morning Jenny and the children looked as if they might cry. "I have a surprise," Josh said. "I have made plans for you to fly out and meet my ship in two months. Study your maps and GUESS where it will be." No one cried. They laughed and hugged and kissed one another.

"One last thing," Jenny said seriously. "Don't forget to call us as soon as you get aboard ship."

"I won't forget," the captain promised.

Cap'n Josh arrived at the San Francisco airport, loaded his bags into a taxi and said to the driver, "My plane was delayed. I will be late getting to my ship unless you can find a shortcut to the pier." Ship captains are famous for being on time – it is very important in their line of work.

The driver said, "Aye, aye, captain," and off they sped.

Who at that moment would have guessed that Cap'n Joshua would not reach his ship on time? No one – least of all Cap'n Joshua and the S.S. HAPPINESS crew.

As the taxi was coming into the city, the driver turned off onto a side street, and Cap'n Josh thought, "That's smart—less traffic this way." He leaned back comfortably, thinking about the things he had to do before his ship sailed at sunset.

Then, suddenly, the taxi SCREECHED to a stop, and Joshua was upside down in the front seat. He turned himself right side up and looked out to see what had happened. "OH, NO," he gasped. "QUICK. LET ME OUT OF THIS TAXI!"

It is two hours later.

Wrecker Raccoon, Chief Engineer of the S.S. HAPPINESS, is deep below decks pacing nervously around his engine room, loosening this valve and tightening that bolt.

"The captain should have been on board two hours ago." (Wrecker is so upset he is talking to himself.) "Something must have happened or he would be here by now. I'm going up to the radio room to see if there has been any message."

Up the stairs he runs...

He flings open the door to the top deck and bumps right into Jack
Rabbit who is jogging around the deck.

"WHOOPS! Sorry," cries Jack, as the two untangle themselves.

"Me, too—I'm heading for the radio room to see if there has been
any message from Cap'n Joshua. He is very late, and I'm WORRIED!"

"So am I," says Jack, frowning. "This is the first time I have had
the job of Sports Director aboard a ship, but I have been a passenger
enough times to know that a captain is NEVER late. LET'S GO!"

9

As they pass the door to the ship hospital, Dr. Phineas sees them
and calls, "Wait a minute—have you seen the captain?
He should have been aboard two hours ago!"

Wrecker looks unhappy. "No one has seen Cap'n Josh. Come with
us! There may be a message from him."

They rush into the radio room and find Tasha, the cruise Entertainment Director. "You all look worried," she says, looking every bit as worried as the other members of the crew. "If you have come to see if the captain has called, he HASN'T. But his wife HAS. She is afraid something TERRIBLE has happened to Cap'n Josh!"

Wrecker, trying to make everyone feel better, says, "Cap'n Josh is as smart as they come and can handle just about any problem there is."

"Quite right," Dr. Phineas agrees. "But what if this is the ONE problem he CAN'T handle? How can we sail without a captain? We would crash into the Golden Gate Bridge before we got to the ocean. This is TERRIBLE, TERRIBLE!"

"Captain Joshua must surely have met with disaster! If I were late getting someplace important like this, it would be because of some horrible disaster—like an earthquake or a flood. Or I might be caught in a stalled elevator. It frightens me to think about all the disasters that COULD get in my way." Dr. Phineas is REALLY upset.

Jack pats the doctor on the back to calm him.
"Don't be so gloomy, Dr. Phineas. Disasters are not
the only things that make folks late. Sometimes I'm late because I'm
having a good time and forget to look at my watch, like when I'm at the
auto races." Jack stares off into the distance and he imagines that
he sees cars roaring around a racecourse.

14

He imagines himself in one of the
fast, powerful cars—pulling into the lead
—crossing the finish line—winning a
big silver trophy. Jack is grinning
happily when Tasha interrupts
his daydream....

15

"I am a little like Jack, myself," Tasha says, "I don't think about disasters very much. If I had been late getting to the ship today, you could blame just one thing— the ballet. Knowing I was going on a voyage that would last six months, I might have gone to one last ballet performance. I would sit in the audience and pretend that I was the star on the stage— just as I used to be. The audience would shout, 'BRAVO, TASHA!— ENCORE, ENCORE!', and people would throw carloads of flowers onto the stage." Tasha is smiling and her eyes are shining. She has forgotten about her missing captain, until Wrecker says…

ENCORE!

42

43

16

"Well, I would have a better excuse than any of you if I were late. If I had needed to catch a plane today like Cap'n Josh did, I would have ended up on the wrong one.

18

There's so much noise and confusion in airports
these days, it would be pretty easy for me
to get mixed up and land in Alaska instead of San Francisco.
I would be stranded with the Eskimos and polar bears.
It makes me SHIVER to think about it."

19

"Enough of this silly chatter," scolds Dr. Phineas. "Cap'n Joshua is not shivering with the polar bears or daydreaming about the auto races or the ballet. There is no news of earthquakes, floods or other disasters. So-oo-o, WHAT in the world has happened to our captain? WHY IS HE MISSING?"

Actually, Cap'n Josh ISN'T
MISSING—not for some people,
anyway. But, WHY isn't he aboard
his ship getting ready to sail just as
he had been planning two hours earlier
when he was thrown into the front seat
and cried, "LET ME OUT OF THIS TAXI!"?

21

It was then that Cap'n Josh had flung open the taxi door, leaped out and raced toward the entrance to a tall building. Smoke was pouring from many of the windows. People in front of the building were looking up, shouting and waving their arms.
It had taken only a second for sharp-eyed Josh to spot the two children calling for help from a window high up in the old, empty building.

Josh could see that the fire had just broken out. No fire trucks or rescue squads had yet arrived. He could see that there was no time to waste.
HE DASHED INTO THE BURNING BUILDING.

Josh knew rescue workers and firemen are allowed to use elevators during a fire, although other people may not, so he pressed the elevator button. Nothing happened. He gasped, "OH, NO–OO–O! The power is off!"

He whirled around, saw a door to the stairway and took off up the stairs two at a time. Josh knew he had to reach the children and bring them down before the stairway filled with smoke and flames.

STAIRWAY →

Thick smoke was gathering in the stairway. Cap'n Josh coughed and coughed, and his eyes stung so that tears ran down his cheeks.

Up, up, up, he struggled, headed for the twelfth floor. On, on, on, he pushed. As he reached the tenth floor he ran head-on into the frightened children as they were plunging down the stairs.

He caught them in his arms. "STOP," he shouted. "We can't get down that way, the smoke is too thick. We must head for the roof before the smoke rises any more." Back up they stumbled, coughing and choking as they struggled through the nasty smoke. It seemed the stairway had no end. At last, there was the door to the roof.

"NOW WE WILL BE SAFE," Josh cried.

But he thought, "only for a little while!"

Grabbing the children by the hand, Josh ran to the edge of the roof, pulled off his coat and waved it at the crowd below.

Six fire trucks were there and he could hear the blaring of sirens as more trucks came nearer and nearer. Jets of water streamed into the windows, but they didn't reach as high as the roof. Ladders were being raised in case there was anyone to rescue on the lower floors. But Cap'n Josh knew there were no ladders that could reach to the roof. And he had seen that the fire escape was rusty and unsafe. They were STRANDED!

"What can I do," he thought. "If we can't get down the stairs, there is NO ESCAPE!" Cap'n Joshua was terribly worried now.

27

Then Josh saw wisps of smoke creeping out from under the stairway door. "It's getting WORSE," he thought. "I must do SOMETHING before it's too late."

The children were waving their sweaters at the firemen below. "Brave kids!" Josh said to himself. "They think I can rescue them. I wish I could—but HOW?"

Josh and the children watched the firemen rushing around far below. The fire chief yelled into a loudspeaker: "STAY CALM—WE WILL SAVE YOU— JUST STAY CALM!"

Firemen carrying axes and hoses ran into the building just as Cap'n Joshua had done. "HOORAY, HERE THEY COME TO SAVE US," cried the children. Josh was afraid the smoke was too thick and the flames too hot for the firemen to make it up the stairway. He was trying not to look worried—BUT IT WAS NOT EASY!

After ten minutes the firemen ran out of the building. "WHY AREN'T THEY COMING TO SAVE US?" cried the children, who were scared and ready to cry.

"HANG ON!" It was the fire chief again. "HELP IS ON THE WAY!" Crowds of people had come to see the fire. Policemen worked hard to keep them out of the way. Wailing blasts of WHOO-EE–WHOO-EE–WHOO-EE came from all directions. Cap'n Joshua couldn't figure out where help could be coming from–but SOMETHING had to be done FAST!

Cap'n Josh wished he had his binoculars so he could get a closer look at the rescue operation below. He wondered if the children could jump from the roof into a net. He decided they might, because kids are sometimes braver than grown-ups. "But it doesn't matter anyway," Josh thought. "We are too high up to jump into a net. Whatever it is they are planning down there, they MUST HURRY!"

Cap'n Josh didn't want his young friends to see the smoke pouring out thicker and blacker from under the stairway door, so he looked up into the sky, smiled as cheerfully as he could, and shouted "I WISH IT WOULD..." Before he could say the word "RAIN," he stopped, stared, began to wave his arms over his head and cried, "LOOK! LOOK AT THAT! HELP IS ON THE WAY! Now that HAS to be the most beautiful big bird I have ever seen anywhere—anytime!"

The children's eyes opened wide and so did their mouths. They began to laugh and jump up and down with happiness for...

33

COMING TOWARDS THEM WAS A HELICOPTER!

"HURRY! HURRY! HURRY!" Josh cried.
Flames were bursting from the windows one floor below them.
THERE WAS NOT ONE SECOND TO WASTE!

The helicopter came closer and closer–CHOP, CHOP, CHOP.
Lower and lower it dropped until it hovered just over the roof.
Cap'n Joshua and the children clapped their hands over their ears to
block out the noise, and they almost toppled over in the strong wind
made by the rotor blades. Then the pilot dropped a rope ladder to the
floor of the roof and shouted, "CLIMB, CLIMB–QUICKLY, QUICKLY!"

The pilot radioed a message that everyone was safe. Fifteen minutes later they landed on the roof of a tall building in the center of the city. Crowds of reporters and television cameramen were waiting. Everyone pushed and shoved around Josh and the children, snapping pictures, shouting questions and poking microphones in their faces. Josh thought, "It could take longer to get away from this roof and this excited crowd than it did from the roof of the burning building."

But AT LAST it was over! The children were in the police chief's
car—sirens blaring—heading back to their happy parents. And...
Josh was in the fire chief's car speeding toward the S.S. HAPPINESS.
Autos, people, trucks and buses hurried out of the way of the
chief's siren. Cap'n Joshua grinned and thought, "Such a fuss over
a sea captain!"

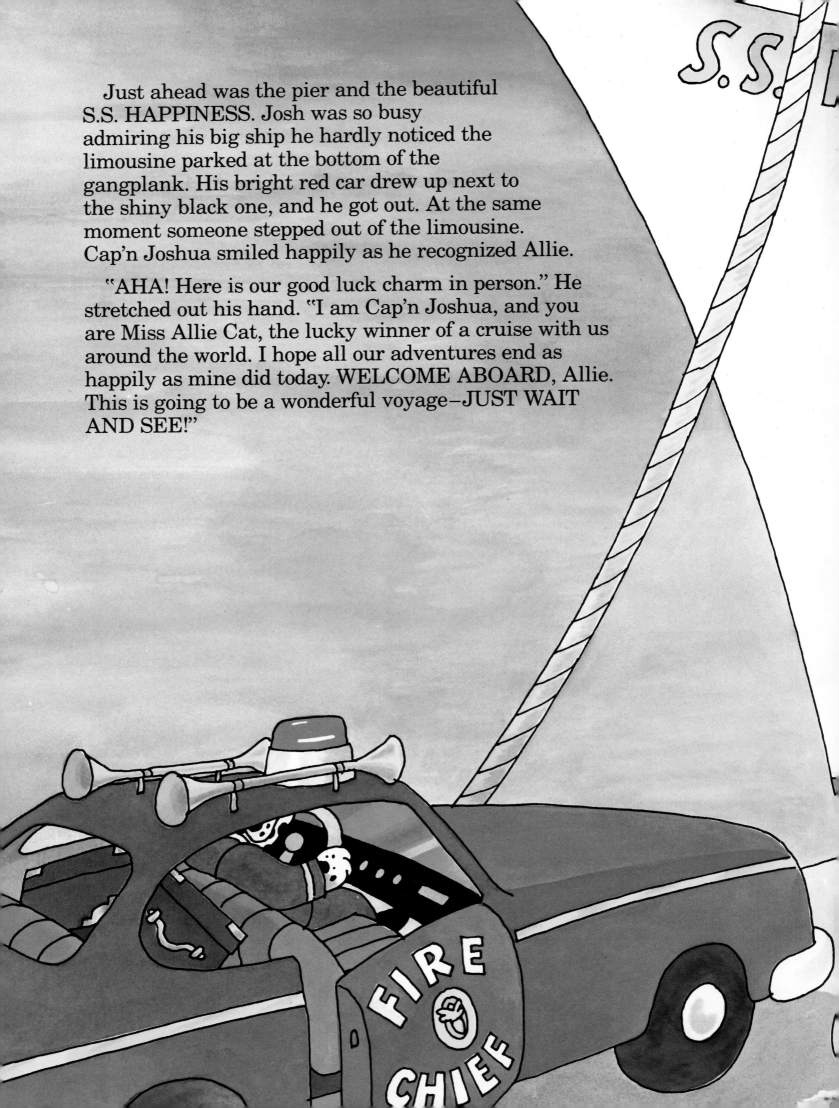

Just ahead was the pier and the beautiful S.S. HAPPINESS. Josh was so busy admiring his big ship he hardly noticed the limousine parked at the bottom of the gangplank. His bright red car drew up next to the shiny black one, and he got out. At the same moment someone stepped out of the limousine. Cap'n Joshua smiled happily as he recognized Allie.

"AHA! Here is our good luck charm in person." He stretched out his hand. "I am Cap'n Joshua, and you are Miss Allie Cat, the lucky winner of a cruise with us around the world. I hope all our adventures end as happily as mine did today. WELCOME ABOARD, Allie. This is going to be a wonderful voyage—JUST WAIT AND SEE!"

APPINESS

CAPT.
JOSHU

43

Exactly on schedule, just as the sun began to set, the S.S. HAPPINESS was ready to sail. Passengers lined the rails shouting, laughing, waving, blowing horns and kisses, tossing streamers and confetti. A long, low blast came from high up in the smoke stack. The S.S. HAPPINESS pulled slowly away from the pier—out into San Francisco Bay toward the Golden Gate—and set her course for China.

★ ★ ★

But who aboard the S.S. HAPPINESS would have guessed that this was ONLY THE BEGINNING—the beginning of a series of the MOST EXCITING adventures of their lives?

45

BE SURE TO WATCH FOR THE NEXT THRILLING
ADVENTURE OF THE S.S. HAPPINESS. CAP'N JOSHUA,
TASHA, WRECKER, JACK, DR. PHINEAS AND ALLIE
WILL ALL BE BACK, ALONG WITH SOME SURPRISING
NEW FRIENDS.

All of your S.S. HAPPINESS friends are available at your favorite gift or department store.
For further information, write to:
Determined Productions, Inc., Box 2150, San Francisco, California 94126.